THE MARTYRDOM OF A PEOPLE

"Others had trial of cruel mockings
and scourgings, yea, moreover of bonds and
imprisonment: They were stoned, they were sawn
asunder, were tempted, were slain with the sword: they
wandered about in sheepskins and goatskins; being
destitute, afflicted, tormented; (of whom the
world was not worthy) they wandered in
deserts, and in mountains, and in
dens and caves of the earth."

Hebrews 11:36–38

THE
MARTYRDOM
OF A PEOPLE

or

The Vaudois of Piedmont and their History

by Henry Fliedner

**Translated from the German by
Constance Cheyne Brady**

from the
1914 Edition

Christian History and Martyrology
Illustrated with thirty-four illustrations
and photographs

Hail & Fire
www.hailandfire.com

"The Martyrdom of a People: or, The Vaudois of Piedmont and their History," by Henry Fliedner, 1914 Edition, translated from the German by Constance Cheyne Brady, is herein updated—in which illustration editing, spelling, grammar, and formatting changes have been made—and reprinted by Hail & Fire.

ISBN 978-0-9828043-0-8

Hail & Fire is a resource for Reformed and Gospel Theology in the works, exhortations, prayers, and apologetics of those who have maintained the Gospel and expounded upon the Scripture as the Eternal Word of God and the sole authority in Christian doctrine. Visit us online at:
www.hailandfire.com

*For posterity, but
most especially for the
children of God*

CONTENTS

LIST OF
ILLUSTRATIONS

"By manifestation of the truth commending ourselves to
every man's conscience in the sight of God."
2 Corinthians 3:2

HAIL & FIRE
REPRINTS

Hail & Fire is a resource for Reformed and Gospel Theology in the works, exhortations, prayers, and apologetics of those who have maintained the Gospel and expounded upon the Scripture as the Eternal Word of God and the sole authority in Christian doctrine.

For the edification of those who believe the Gospel in truth and for the examination of all consciences, Hail & Fire reprints and republishes, in print and online, Christian, Puritan, Reformed and Protestant sermons and exhortative works; Protestant and Catholic polemical and apologetical works; Bibles, histories, martyrologies, and eschatological works.

Visit us online at:
www.hailandfire.com

PREFACE

Having for many years taken a deep interest in the history of the Waldenses, having also read extensively on the subject, and visited the beautiful Valleys of the Vaudois, I have read Dr. Fliedner's Martyrdom of a People with peculiar interest and pleasure. It is a story which should fascinate both old and young, and none can read without profit about the persecutions and sufferings of the noble people who, for so many centuries, kept the torch of truth burning brightly in the midst of popish darkness.

Dr. Fliedner, I see, adopts the theory that the Waldenses were descended from the "Poor Men of Lyons," the followers of Peter Waldo. This is the view taken by many writers on the Waldenses, but it is only right to mention that some authorities do not agree with this view. There are some other points in the historical statements made by Dr. Fliedner which are not beyond doubt, as authorities differ in regard to these, but the whole story seems to me to be substantially correct, and I hope it will do much to create and sustain interest in this remarkable people, who feel that they have been preserved by God in a miraculous way for a great purpose, and that nothing less than the evangelization of Italy; to this task they are setting themselves right heartily.

J. Forbes Moncrieff, 1914

The Martyrdom of a People

OR

The Vaudois of Piedmont and their History

Introduction

Most people have heard something of the Vaudois or Waldenses, but the origin, manners, and customs, and the history of this singular people, are little enough known, although they merit the warmest sympathy of the evangelical world. Even "De Amicis," a Roman Catholic writer, confesses the same conviction. He introduces his very comprehensive history of the Vaudois by a masterly sketch, which involuntarily transforms itself into a panegyric to the glory of these faithful witnesses of Jesus Christ.

"Let us penetrate into this glorious and celebrated region—this little Switzerland, of which Torre Pellice will answer for Geneva—into the midst of a strange people which form, as it were, a nation in itself. Dwelling in the elevated valleys, situated on the upper reaches of the Po, and the valley of Susa, this people, whose origin is lost in the mist of ages, has a religion of its own, an original language and literature, as well as an independent religious constitution.

"Notwithstanding their small number, they have connections and colonies all over Italy, as well as in Germany and America. They can boast of friendship with peoples and princes. Admirers and friends from every country go to visit them, and they send out pioneers of the Gospel and missionaries to 'the regions beyond.'

"In their own Valleys of Piedmont, the Vaudois never surpassed the number of twenty thousand, and these are distributed over fifteen parishes. In spite of this they have known the vicissitudes of a great people, and have shown their strength. They have had their armies, their captains, their heroes, and their martyrs. Once and again they entered into treaty with the great country of which they form a small part, and more than thirty times they fought against it, sometimes against Piedmont, sometimes against France, and often against the two powers united.

"Like the Israelites, they were torn from their country, and they reconquered it; dispersed, decimated, nearly annihilated as an accursed race of whom the earth needed to be purged, yet they arose again in greater numbers, and stronger than before. Their invincible tenacity at last wore out their oppressors. After that they fought for their common country, Italy, side by side with their former adversaries, who were constrained to grant them liberty, and to be ashamed of the past.

"Notwithstanding their many persecutions, which might well have broken all the ties that united them to their country, they always remained Italians at heart. At the present time they are as loyal to United Italy as they were in the past to Piedmont, and form one of her most patriotic provinces; therefore let us give all due honor to the Vaudois."

I.

ORIGIN OF THE VAUDOIS

I.
Origin of the Vaudois

"The wind bloweth where it listeth and thou hearest the sound thereof, but canst not tell whence it cometh and whither it goeth, so is every one that is born of the Spirit." These words of Jesus came into my mind as I was searching ancient books for the origin of the Vaudois. For no one will ever know exactly where they came from.

The generally accepted tradition that *Peter Valdus*, the pious merchant of Lyons, was the founder of the Vaudois Church is doubted by many scholars. Their name seems to be derived from the Latin, *Vallis* or *Valley*, so that Vaudois would signify people, or inhabitants of the valley. There are other indications which allow of the supposition that, long before the time of Peter Valdus, there were in this part of the Alps, and in many districts in the north of Italy, associations which opposed the superstitions and the abuses of the dominant church, and remained true to the pure faith founded on the Bible.

1

Monte Viso and the Lake of Florenzo.

These retired valleys of the western Alps extending eastward from the mountains Cenis and Viso, where lie the Val Cluson with the Germanasco, and the Val Pelis, are still at the present time quite separated from the rest of the world; and those who traverse them understand why here, rather than in any other place, an Apostolic simplicity should have been preserved, both in doctrine and in customs. In fact, the inhabitants are hostile to innovations. They hold to their old customs, and to their ancient garb, with a tenacity which reminds one of the granite of their mountains.

To the above one should add that, just at the commencement of the middle ages, when the Christian Church was rapidly being transformed into a Papal Church, there was at Turin a man who opposed the invading corruption with all his power. This was Claudius, Archbishop of Turin.

Typical Vaudois Apparel.

The Emperor Louis, the pious son and successor of Charlemagne, had raised Claudius from the dignity of Court Chaplain to the Archiepiscopal seat, that he might use his influence, being well versed in the Scriptures, against the growing superstitions of the Italian people.

This he did with great spiritual force, both by word and by his pen. "If," he insisted, "those who have abandoned the worship of idols venerate the images of saints, they have not forsaken idolatry, but they have only changed the label. Whoever does not show the faith and virtue by which the Saints became pleasing to God, he cannot be saved." By such-like incisive and truly evangelical words, he combated the worship of saints and the adoration of images. "If one adores all wood in the form of a cross, because Christ was crucified, one should adore all mangers because Jesus was placed in one; one should also adore asses, because Jesus rode on one; and the same with boats, since often He spoke to the people from a boat. We have not received a command to worship the cross, but to carry it and to deny ourselves." He opposed the arrogance of the Pope, who caused himself to be addressed 'Apostolic Lord,' and the pilgrimages to Rome, which had no other reason than a misconception of the words of Christ, "Thou art Peter, and on this rock I will build My church."

One can easily understand that this reforming zeal brought much enmity and annoyance to the devoted Archbishop. He lamented it, and said, "Whosoever catches sight of me, mocks me and points the finger at me. When I was forced to take the responsibility of a pastor on my arrival in Italy, I found, contrary to the true doctrine, the churches filled with the refuse of ex-votos.

As I, quite alone, set myself to destroy that which all venerated, I was slandered by all; if the Lord had not come to my aid, they would have swallowed me up alive. The Father of mercies and consolation strengthened me in my misery; by Him I was sustained in all my trials, armed with the armor of Divine justice, and protected by the helmet of salvation."

If, on one side, Claudius of Turin had to suffer persecution and shame, without doubt the example and words of a prince of the Church must have contributed in a large measure to fortify the Vaudois and all those in his diocese, who, like him, fought against the dominant abuses, all the more that he was not content with

Typical Vaudois Apparel.

protesting, but applied himself to explain the Bible to the people. And it was not in vain. Later Roman Catholic historians complained that his errors were propagated by his disciples. These complaints reappeared each century

in the north-western part of Italy. In 1028 they even brought an accusation of heresy against an entire parish, that of Monforte, near Albi. We shall not err in seeing in these so-called arch-heretics the fathers and forerunners of the present Vaudois. Unfortunately, certain information of these distant times has not come down to us. On the other hand, we possess a precious document, a kind of confession of faith, known by the name of "La Noble Leçon."

Though in its present form it is comparatively recent, it may be presumed that in substance it gives the doctrines which were from ancient times familiar to the Vaudois.

The illustrations on pages 7 and 9 are reproductions of two pages of the most ancient manuscripts of "La Noble Leçon," which are preserved in the library of the University of Cambridge, where they were placed in the time of Oliver Cromwell. Here are the principal sentences:

"Oh brothers, listen to a noble lesson;

We must watch, and be diligent in prayer,

Because we see the world is approaching its end.

Already eleven hundred years have run their course

Since it was written, 'these are the last times.'

But no man will know, when the end is to come.

We have all the more to fear. We do not know

If death will call us today or tomorrow.

But when Christ comes on the Day of Judgment

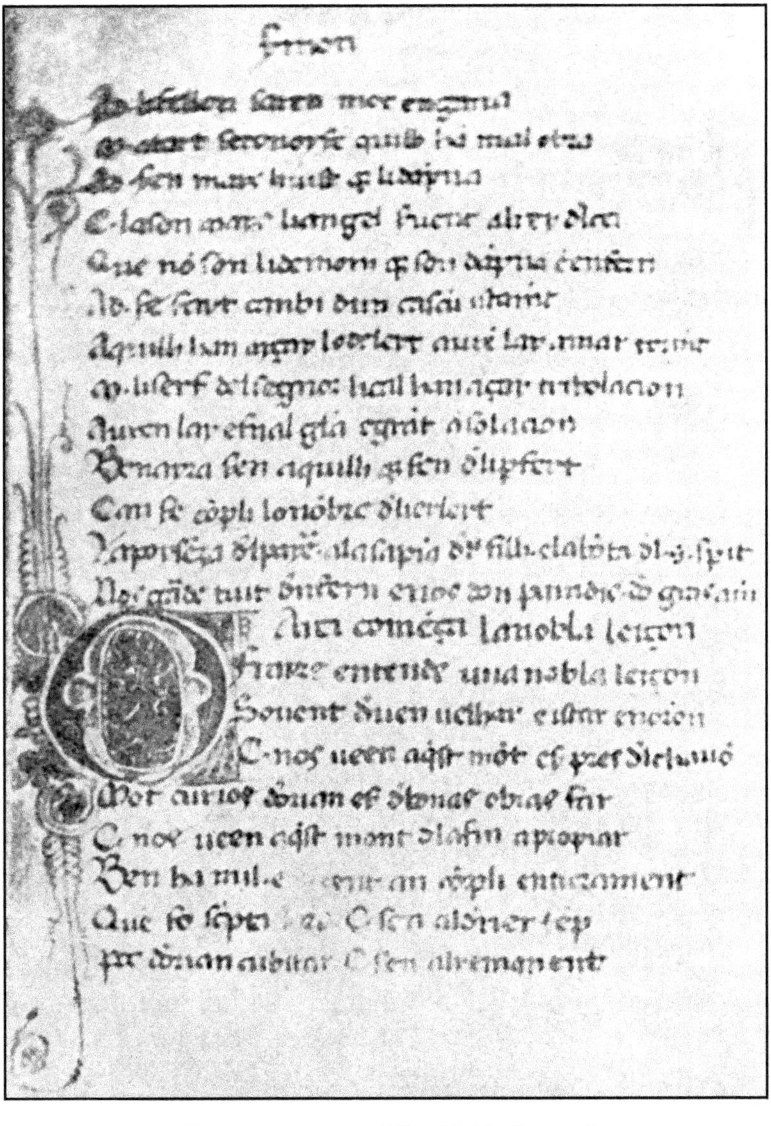

Commencement of "La Noble Leçon."

Each will receive his reward;

As well, he who has done evil as he who has done good.

If we desire to love Christ and learn His doctrine

We must watch and search the Scriptures.

If we read them, we shall find,

That Christ was persecuted because He did good.

There are still many in our times

Who wish to teach the way of Christ,

But they are persecuted and can do but little.

False Christians are so blinded by error,

And particularly the teachers themselves,

That they ill-use and kill those who are better than themselves.

On the contrary they let the evil live in peace.

By this we may know that they are not good shepherds,

They love the sheep only for their wool.

If anyone loves God, and fears Jesus Christ,

And does not bear false witness, nor swear nor lie,

And does not commit adultery, nor kill, nor does violence,

Nor revenge himself on his enemies,

They say, 'He is a Vaudois; he merits death!'

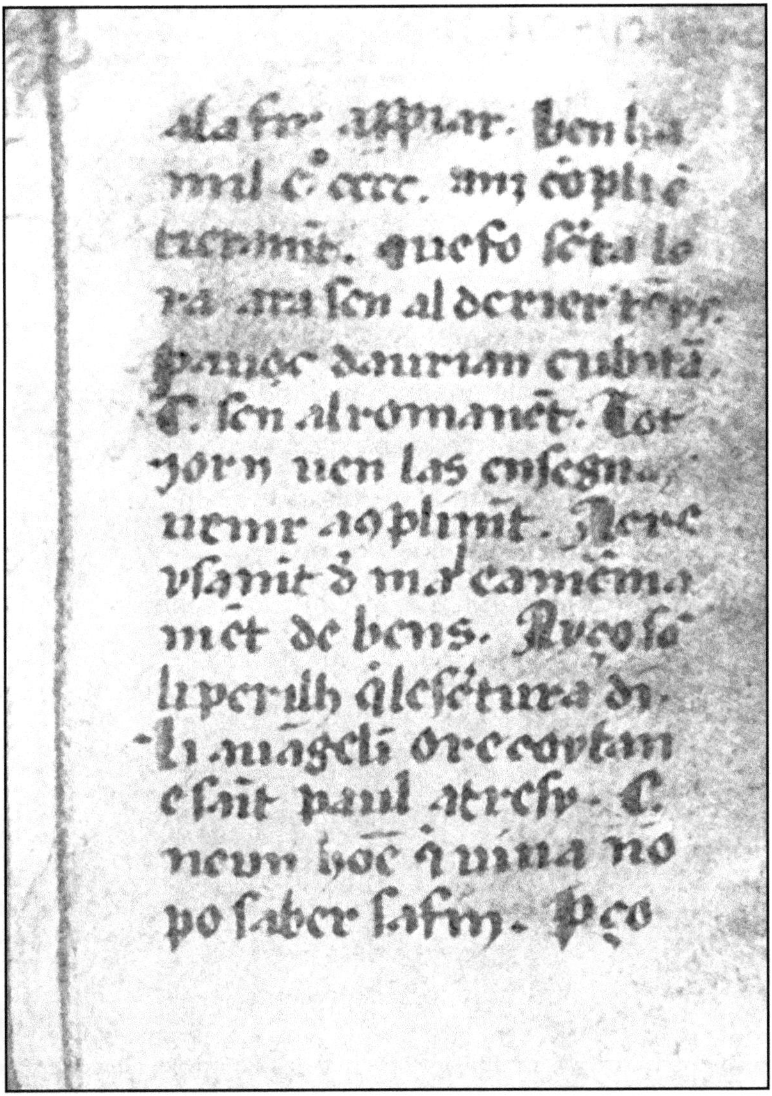
a la fin apparelhar. Ben ha
mil e cccc. anz compli e
tierament. que fo scripta lo
ra. car sen al derier temp
Pauc deurian cubitar
E. sen al romanent. Tot
jorn uen las ensegna
uenir a compliment. Acre
yssament de mal e amermament
ment de bens. Aiço son
li peril lh ql escriptura di
li euangeli o recontan
e sant paul atresi. E
neun home que uiua no
po saber la fin. Per ço

A page from the Cambridge Manuscript.

But he who is persecuted, because he fears God,

Can console himself, for after he leaves this world,

Heaven will open to him its doors.

And there, instead of shame, he will enjoy great honor.

This I dare to say, and the people will see that it is the truth,

All the popes, from Sylvestre* to our days,

All the cardinals, archbishops, and abbots united,

Have not the power to absolve anyone,

Nor grant him pardon for his mortal sins.

God alone pardons, and no one else.

On the other hand, the duty of the teachers

Is to pray, and to preach to the people;

To nourish them often by the word of God;

With a sound reprimand to punish sinners,

And to exhort them to repentance by serious remonstrances,

So that they may follow the Lord Jesus, and do His will,

And hold faithfully to His precepts."

* Pope Sylvestre was Bishop of Rome in the 4th century, and it was he, according to the Vaudois, who commenced to corrupt the Church.

II.

PETER VALDUS AND THE "POOR MEN OF LYONS"

Petrus Valdus, from Luther's Monument at Worms.

II.

Peter Valdus and the "Poor Men of Lyons"

he town of Lyons was, at the end of the 12th century, the scene of a powerful religious revival, the initiator of which was the rich merchant Peter, whose surname Valdus is probably derived from his native place Vaux, or Vallis.

This merchant resembled the merchantman in the Gospels who went seeking for pearls, who, when he had found one pearl of great price, went and sold all that he had and bought it. Peter Valdus' heart was not set on the earthly riches, which God had allotted to him in abundance, but he applied himself to acquire spiritual treasures, "which neither moth nor rust doth corrupt."

God made him, as he made Luther, pass through a special school. He happened one day to be in the society of a number of friends and acquaintances, when one of them suddenly fell down dead, as if he had been struck by lightning. Profoundly agitated, Valdus asked himself, "Where should I have been now, if it had been me, whom death had struck down?" The thought of death, judgment, and eternity did not leave him from that time. He sought with new zeal the salvation of his soul, and God, who is beforehand with those who seek, guided his anxious soul to the desired haven.

In reading religious books, the works of the Fathers of the Church, he obtained the certainty, then uncommon, that the Word of God is the true source of the Christian Faith. From that time he had no rest till he could get access to this source, but then it was less easy than it is at present, when one can procure the sacred volume for a few pence.

The Bible was only to be obtained in Latin, and this language Valdus did not understand. He succeeded, nevertheless, since "where there is a will there is a way." He was acquainted with two pious priests, whose names we know; one was Etienne de Ansa, and the other, Bernard Ydros. They were both clever Latin scholars, and were more versed than their contemporaries in the knowledge of the Scriptures. Together they set to work and translated the Gospels for Peter Valdus. Etienne, the more learned, dictated, and Bernard, who was an excellent copyist, soon had it put down in writing. One after another all the books of the Bible passed through their hands.

Valdus rejoiced at last to be able to read, without difficulty, the wonderful words of Jesus, His parables, and the record of His miracles. We cannot have an idea of this man's delight, we who from our infancy have been privileged to possess the Bible. He did not regret the great sum he had to pay the two priests. Far from it. Now that he had found the pearl of great price, that he had seen its beauty, and estimated its value, he would not keep his treasure for his own benefit, but burned to share it with others. Therefore he consecrated a great part of his fortune to the spread of the Word of God—which had given him happiness—among his fellow citizens.

Before the discovery of printing, books were very costly, because they had to be entirely written by hand, and those who undertook this work were few in number. A Bible then cost many pounds, and it was a large, unwieldy volume.

Valdus had several Gospels and Books copied separately, but his great aim was to spread the Word by preaching. He invited his friends to his house, reading to them part of these books, and explaining them, as well as his studies and prayers permitted him, with the help of the Holy Spirit.

These Bible meetings attracted more and more people. One room after another was filled with auditors, and when there was no more room in the house, the people invaded the street, so anxious were they to hear the message which the Church refused to let them have. The fire of divine love kindled their hearts by the preaching of Valdus, and spread from place to place. Some friends associated themselves with him in carrying the Gospel to the towns and villages in the neighborhood. They went as missionaries, and were everywhere received with enthusiasm. The words of their lips were confirmed by the testimony of their lives. While the Roman priests were living in luxury and pleasures, Valdus and his companions faithfully imitated Jesus Christ, who was poor; they gave all they had to the needy, and, travelling through the country like poor people, lived strictly according to the precepts of Jesus.

The enmity of the clergy became stronger as the attendance of the people increased at the preaching. At first they had mocked and treated them with contempt, as dreamers of strange things; then the Archbishop of Lyons, in severe terms, forbade them all ecclesiastical activity, under the pretext that the preaching and explanation of the Bible was forbidden to the laity, and was the exclusive department of the priests.

Until this moment Valdus had been a faithful son of the Church, though his desire had been to make up for her deficiencies as far as he could by his unpretending efforts. He could not, however, obey the injunctions of the Archbishop, because he had read Christ's command, "Go ye, therefore, and teach all nations." Since the clergy did not obey this command, he considered himself authorized, nay, even called of God to fulfill it. However, he tried to avoid an open rupture with the Church.

With this object he sent some of the most faithful believers to Rome to appeal to the Pope on the subject of the Episcopal decree. At Rome they went through the same experience as did Luther several centuries later. The question was submitted to a council then sitting in the Eternal City, and the friends of Valdus laid before it their translation of the Bible. To all the pointed questions, which were put to them, they knew what to say, and replied so well to their adversaries, by quoting passages of the Scriptures, that their principal opponent, a monk named Gautier Mapes, was reduced to silence. His inability to refute them made him extremely angry. He was obliged to acknowledge their apostolical methods, and to pay them a tribute of admiration. "They have no settled home," he said, "but travel two and two, barefooted and clothed in woolen garments; they possess nothing, but have everything in common like the Apostles; deprived of everything, they follow Christ, who gave up all." At the same time he perceived the superiority of their preaching, and asked the council not to give their approval, nor to allow them liberty of speech. "They are now commencing in a most humble manner, because they have not yet gained a footing, but if we allow them to become established, we ourselves will soon be chased by them out of the Church." This warning, unhappily, had such an effect on the majority of the Bishops that they flatly refused to grant the authorization demanded by the deputies, who were enjoined to submit to the orders of the Archbishop.

The moment had now come, when Valdus and his followers saw they must obey God rather than man. They neither could nor would abstain from witnessing to that which had become the consolation of their hearts and the joy of their souls. When the Archbishop chased them from Lyons, they went into all the other counties, and the same things took place as in Apostolic times after the martyrdom of Stephen, namely, "a great number believed, and were converted to the Lord." Soon, in Provence, Dauphiné, and in the south, one heard nothing else talked of but the Gospel. The people listened to the new doctrine all the more readily knowing it was the Gospel, and because the Church had fallen into contempt, and was displeasing to the people, the opposition of the clergy being ineffectual. Peter Valdus, as leader of the movement, was naturally more exposed than others to persecution. He obeyed the Master's command: "When they persecute you in this city, flee ye to another."

From this time it is difficult to follow his track. He seems to have crossed the Alps, returned into the north of Italy, and from there he must have gone to Germany, and finally to Bohemia. In any case we find traces of the activity of the Vaudois on the borders of the Rhine, in Bohemia, and Moravia, where they formed the Church of the Moravian Brethren.

Truly the hand of the Lord was with this poor little flock of faithful confessors. The "Poor Men of Lyons," as they were called in France, made a great number rich. Though they were simple people, and went like sheep among wolves, they sought to be wise as serpents.

An old chronicler gives us a living picture of their mode of working. "They often travelled on horseback in different countries as hawkers, and, thanks to their bales of goods, obtained access to the rich and poor. When they entered a house, they would humbly ask, 'Do you wish to buy a ring, some cloth, or embroidery?' While the merchant was doing business, he would observe the character of his customers, and when, at the end, they asked if he had anything else to sell, he would reply, 'Certainly, I have treasures much more precious than those which you have seen, and I am inclined to acquaint you with them, if you will promise not to denounce me to the priests.' In most cases the promise was given, because the priests were detested on account of their thirst for domination, and their vices. The Vaudois would then continue, 'We possess a jewel which shines with such brightness, that it enables one to see, and to come to the knowledge of God; it gives out such heat that it sets the heart on fire with love to God. The inestimable treasure of which I speak is the Word, which God has revealed to us by a manifestation of His will.' The merchant then drew out of his pocket, or from a secret drawer of his travelling chest, a Gospel, and commenced to read a portion, such as the Sermon on the Mount, the Parable of the Sower, or the Good Samaritan. The people listened intently, because it was absolutely new to them. The foreign merchant soon became a guest beloved, whom they constrained to stay with them longer, so as to hear more, and to become enriched with these hidden treasures."

In this way the Vaudois found a means of spreading the Word of God more and more. It is asserted that they could travel from Milan to Cologne, sleeping each night in the house of a co-religionist. What wonderful results might this seed-time have produced, if the storm of persecution had not broken out, reducing almost to naught the people of God.

The Vaudois Merchant, reading Scripture aloud.

III.

THE FIRST PERSECUTIONS

III.
The First Persecutions

bout the commencement of the 13th century the "Poor Men of Lyons," or the Vaudois, and the other evangelical sects, had spread so much in the south of France that the Roman Church was in fear of losing all authority over the people. This was during the rule of Pope Innocent III, one of the most energetic and powerful pontiffs the Church had ever produced. He had so much power and influence over the whole of Europe that he could establish or depose kings and princes at his own good pleasure. He had the wisdom to perceive that his predecessors committed a great mistake in breaking with the Vaudois, instead of gaining them, and turning to the service of the Church their strength, enthusiasm, and their devotion. He tried to repair this error, and enlist them by the mediation of devout legates, and to make them a regular community in the Church: a sort of begging and preaching order which would continue to work under the direction of the Pope.

The proposal was seductive. At a stroke the "Poor Men of Lyons" or the Vaudois would be exempted from all persecution. Above all, they would have enjoyed the favor of an all-powerful Pope, and of the bishops.

Some of them allowed themselves to be tempted by these fallacious offers, but the greater number recognized the danger there was in losing the full truth of the Gospel and their liberty for a few material advantages. The persecutions they had already endured had doubtless, in accord with God's design, opened their eyes to the profoundly rooted corruption in the Roman institution. So they, like their Lord and Master, replied to the tempter, "Get thee behind me, for it is written, 'Thou shalt worship the Lord thy God, and Him only shalt thou serve.'"

When the Pope perceived that his cunning and cleverness had fallen through, he was furiously angry, and determined to exterminate these cursed heretics by fire and sword.

The Pope turned to advantage the fact that in the south of France, besides the "Poor Men of Lyons," whose faith was that of the Bible, there was another sect which had many errors mingled with evangelical truth. According to the reports of their adversaries—assuredly not impartial— they seem to have taught, that beside God, who was good, the Father of our Lord Jesus Christ, there was another and evil divinity. They thought little of marriage, and of the sacraments, and abstained from eating meat. This sect had its seat in the town of Albi, in Languedoc, from which the name Albigenses was given to its adherents.

Roman historians of all times have willfully confounded the Albigenses and the Vaudois, so as to include them both in the same hatred and the same persecutions. At first the Pope tried to induce the princes to persecute the heretics in their countries, and, in particular, the powerful Count Raymond of Toulouse. This latter opposed the project with all his strength, for he would not with his own hands destroy the best and most faithful of his subjects. And as the Pope's Legate arrogantly insisted, he showed him the door, which indeed he had a right to do. Unhappily, one of the Count's knights, wishing to revenge his master's honor, mounted his horse, overtook the Legate, and assassinated him. This bloody deed was doubly welcomed by the Pope, as a pretext to have a crusade preached throughout the whole of France against heretics and assassins. He promised plenary indulgence for every sin, glory and plunder to all who would take part in the crusade.

What are known as The Crusades proper may be looked upon as the most imposing exploits of the Middle Ages, and were undertaken solely to deliver Jerusalem and the Holy Land from the yoke of the Turks. This thought, then, had animated with sacred enthusiasm the entire Christendom of the Occident, and caused thousands on thousands to leave home and family, and risk their lives in harassing warlike expeditions by land and by sea in many bloody battles, for the honor of their Lord and Savior as they believed. But these enormous sacrifices, made by all the Christian nations of the Occident, were rendered in vain. The Holy Land was conquered only to be lost again; yet this holy enthusiasm had not died out, and a crusade seemed still to most Christians the best and holiest deed they could do to ensure their salvation. And now this powerful Pope Innocent had a new crusade preached throughout the Catholic countries against infidels—not against the Turks, but against the heretics in France.

Need we be surprised that this appeal, sent forth into every country by the Pope's legates, priests, and monks, soon gathered together a great company—some say as many as five hundred thousand men—many of whom were filled with burning enthusiasm to fight the heretics; others, no doubt the greater number, were attracted by the prospect of rich spoil. At that time all the south of France resembled a beautiful garden, planted with olive trees and vines, and full of wealthy villages, and nourishing towns.

The Pope nominated the abbot, Arnaud de Citeaux, as the leader of the crusade. We can gain some idea of this man by the words he pronounced during the siege of the town of Bezières. At the assault some soldiers asked him, how they were to distinguish good Catholics from the heretics. The Pope's Legate made this horrible reply, "Kill them all; the Lord will know His own." This sanguinary order was executed to the letter. After the gates were broken and the wall scaled, a fearful butchery began; neither age nor sex was spared. The crowd rushed into the principal church, and cried out for mercy—in vain! The sword did its work with undiscriminating cruelty—men, women, and children were massacred in the nave. In this church alone, seven thousand six hundred men are said to have been slaughtered.

In the same manner the other castles and towns were taken, pillaged, and burnt. At last the country, formerly so flourishing, resembled a desert. Opposition being broken down, the object then was to discover those who secretly adhered to the heresy. The Pope instituted that terrible tribunal of the Inquisition, nominating the Dominicans as judges. They were given such absolute powers that they could summon to their tribunal whoever was suspected of heresy, whether prince, knight, or high dignitary of the Church. They fulfilled their mission with such sanguinary zeal that the people named them "Domini Canes," or the blood-hounds of the Lord.

All who escaped the sword went the way to prison, or died at the stake, unless they managed to find refuge in the ravines and valleys of the Pyrenees, or in the Vaudois Alps. Thus it happened that the inhospitable valleys of the Western Alps, which up to this time were unfrequented, and with few inhabitants, had a considerable number added to their population, while at this same time the rich fields of France became deserted.

From this period the authenticated facts of the Vaudois are more abundant and exact. Communities were formed; for the first time we hear of ecclesiastics called "Barbes," who were also called Uncle, as a sign of filial veneration. These Barbes had little learning, which it would have been difficult for them to acquire in their valleys, but in the Bible they were practiced adepts.

They knew by heart most of the Books of the New Testament, and explained them so well that their hearers would not listen to any other preachers. A celebrated Roman preacher vainly attempted to bring back the simple Vaudois into the bosom of the Church, and to confound the "Barbes" with his learning. His time and trouble were thrown away, for, after several years of continued efforts, he was obliged to return from whence he came, without having succeeded.

The Barbes had no settled dwelling, as have most pastors of the present time, but, like Valdus and his companions, travelled from place to place, often undertaking long journeys to carry the Gospel into countries where as yet it was unknown. They lived on the voluntary gifts of the faithful, and were frugal and simple like the Apostles.

But it was not only the Barbes who taught the Word to the people. One must estimate much more highly the zeal which these poor mountaineers showed in trying to familiarize themselves and their children with the truth. Even Roman Catholic writers recorded their admiration at the diligence with which laborers at their work, mothers with their children, peasant farmers with their maids and men-servants, learned and taught the Gospel. Should someone excuse himself on account of a bad memory, they would reply, "Learn only a few words each day, and at the end of the year you will have amassed a treasure."

Besides the words of the Bible, they willingly taught precepts and proverbs to the young. "Naked and poor we come into the world, naked and poor we leave it." "The beginning and the end of life are the same with the rich and the poor, with the lord and with the servant." "Ingratitude is a wind which dries up the springs of Divine mercy." "A good action is a good prayer." "The lying tongue kills the soul." Precepts like these were easily engrafted in the memory, and transmitted from mouth to mouth, and from generation to generation.

The Vaudois were very tenacious of discipline, and an austere manner of life. They regarded dancing as a gross sin, as also music and the pleasures of the tavern. "God shows His power," they said, "in making cripples to walk, in giving hearing to the deaf, and sight to the blind: in the tavern the devil does just the contrary, because when a drinker leaves the tavern, not only has he lost the power of walking straight, but he has lost hearing, sight, speech, sense, and memory."

When they had differences, they did not take them to tribunals, but submitted them to the judgment of the elders; the wise and just decisions of these men gained them so much consideration that the Catholics themselves submitted to them their difficulties. The

Inquisitor Sachoni gives this testimony to the Vaudois: "The sect of the Vaudois differ totally from the others, who arouse only disgust in those who hear them by their detestable doctrines. This sect leads people astray by a certain appearance of piety. Their adherents live regular lives in public, and believe in regard to God all the articles of the 'Credo,' but they slander the Catholic Church and the Clergy. Their habits are regular and modest. They wear nothing of value. The greater number of them appear to be poor; their women are distinguished by their chastity, avoiding gossip, thoughtless speech, and swearing.

Many of them know the New Testament, and part of the Old by heart, and they do not desire to know anything else, for they say that all that the preachers teach, which they cannot prove by the Bible, is a lie."

It might have been expected that the various counts and lords who ruled the Vaudois Valleys, would have defended from their enemies such faithful and laborious subjects. This some of them did, and viewed without displeasure little bands of the persecuted arrive one after another, from the south of France, and take refuge in these savage Alpine valleys, clear the poor soil, and build villages which are today pretty towns, like Pomaretto, and others, while in the high pasturages they raised cattle, and thus increased the prosperity of the country.

During the 13th and 14th centuries many Inquisitors penetrated to these wild valleys, but of this we do not know much. Towards the year fourteen hundred, we have some details of an attack by a troop of fanatical Catholics, directed by the Inquisitor Borelli, against the peaceable inhabitants of the Pragelas. This elevated valley of the Cottian Alps lies at the foot of the mighty Albergian peak, more than nine thousand feet high. It is so retired and wild that the inhabitants up to the present day travel on foot, or on mules. Therefore the women and children learn to ride as well as the men.

One can hardly imagine what like the mountain paths were in this part five centuries ago, still less the eagerness

Peasants of the Val Pragelas.

of the Inquisitor, whom neither mountains nor snow could arrest. At unawares he fell upon the unsuspecting mountaineers the day before Christmas, and the unhappy people were not able to defend themselves from the sudden attack. The only means of safety was speedy flight into the mountains; so the mothers took their young babes in their arms, and the men, loading themselves with some food, and taking their children by the hand, rushed towards the heights covered with snow and ice. Many of them were overtaken by their pursuers and killed, others wandered about and perished of cold in the snow, among whom there were eighty children. The greater number were able to reach the summit of the mountain, more than nine thousand feet high, called from that time "Albergia," i.e., shelter or asylum.

After this unforeseen storm many long years of peace followed. Then, in 1488, Pope Innocent VIII sent an army against them. This they repulsed so valiantly that it was forced to depart, filled with shame at the want of success.

Claudius de Seyssel, Archbishop of Turin, was a mild and reasonable man, who preferred gentleness to violence as a means of bringing back the wandering sheep into the bosom of the Church. He carefully studied their institutions, customs, and doctrines, and rendered the following testimony: "They observe the laws and Christian ordinances better than many of ourselves, excepting the points in which they differ from the Church. However, their conduct is better than those who call themselves Christians. They swear only when obliged to do so, faithfully keep their word, and live in the greatest simplicity."

One could not have a better testimony to these so-called heretics than this from a prince of the Catholic Church of that time.

IV.

THE VAUDOIS ON THE BORDERS OF THE RHINE

IV.

The Vaudois on the Borders of the Rhine

he zeal of the "Poor men of Lyons" impelled them to go beyond the limits of their country. They obeyed Christ's command to "go into all the world, and preach the Gospel to every creature."Besides this, persecution drove them into places where they were least expected. If some took refuge in the Western Alps, others turned their steps towards the north, Lorraine and Metz, and from there to Treves, and Cologne. Everywhere their exemplary life and evangelical preaching gained them many friends. About the year 1140, the Provost of Steinbach wrote as follows to the Abbot Bernard de Clairvaux:

"Recently, in the neighborhood of Cologne, we have seen certain heretics, some of whom have voluntarily returned to the Church. On the other hand, one of their Bishops dared to speak in an assembly where there was an Archbishop and a great number of nobles. He openly defended his heresy, using the words of Christ and of the

Apostles. They despise earthly grandeur, and aspire to be the foremost in imitating Jesus, so as to form the only true Church of Christ on earth. They endeavor to lead a pure life. They make a great deal of their temperance and the simplicity of their worship, and they compare themselves to the ancient martyrs, who fled from town to town like sheep among wolves. They blame the priests for their worldliness, and call them false prophets, accusing them of having destroyed the Word of God, and for being strangers to the sanctity of their vocation. They consider Purgatory a fable, reject the adoration of saints as blasphemy, and refuse to obey the Pope. In a word, everything in the Church which was not instituted by Christ or the Apostles, they treat as superstition."

One is truly astonished that such a pious and sincere man, as the Prevost de Steinbach seems to have been, could have called such Christians heretics. We are less astonished at the success which the priests achieved over them at Cologne. They succeeded so well in stirring up the hatred of the people against the heretics, that they seized them, and threw them into the flames, with cries of rage.

At Strasburg, the most flourishing of the towns of the Upper Rhine, the citizens were distinguished for their remarkable religious spirit.

At the commencement of the 13th century the Dominicans discovered there a community which resembled, both in their customs and doctrines, the Vaudois of Italy, though they had not taken the name, so as to avoid persecution. The people marked them by the strange nomenclature of "God's Bread," because they gave large gifts to the poor and to beggars, without adding the traditional phrase, "For the love of Peter, and of our Lady," but always said, "For the love of God." By this they showed they did not venerate the saints. This secret community counted five hundred adherents, many of whom were rich and noble. The Bishop of Strasburg did not dare to use violent measures towards them, but first tried by religious discussion to bring them back; however, the Vaudois, knowing their Bible thoroughly, were always able to confound their opponents. Then the prelate had an edict published, that in future all heresy would be suppressed by extreme severity, and those who refused to obey would be sentenced to the stake.

This measure shook many, who craved pardon, gave up their Bibles and religious books, while they also confessed that the community, had three chief men. The first and foremost of these resided at Milan; the second, named Birkhardus, in Bohemia; and the third was Priest John of Strasburg. Immediately this latter was closely interrogated. The judges did not succeed in convicting him of heresy, because he appealed without ceasing to the Word of God. Seeing this, they ordered him to prove the truth of his doctrine by a "Judgment of God," that of the red-hot iron. Priest John replied simply, "It is written, 'Thou shalt not tempt the Lord thy God,' He has given us His word to distinguish what is true and what is false." His enemies then exclaimed, "See! He will not burn his fingers!" "I have the Word of God," replied this witness of Christ, "for it I would not only give my fingers but my entire body to the fire."

And this he did, for the priest John and eighty other unfortunates were condemned to the stake. Before their execution they were informed why they were to be put to death; it was on account of seventeen articles of their doctrines which appeared to be particularly heretical. Here are the most important of them; they prove that those doomed ones were faithful witnesses of Jesus Christ.

"They believe and teach that God should not be worshipped excepting through Jesus Christ, in spirit and in truth. Therefore all images and their adoration should be rejected. This is heresy against the Holy Roman Church and a scandal.

"They do not believe that the Pope is ruler of the entire world, and of all earthly kingdoms, or that he has power to add to, or take from, the Word of God.

"They count auricular confession, absolution, or excommunication useless, because men can deceive and lie. The Pope is also a man, therefore he is fallible. A religious layman is more capable of giving absolution than a bad priest, because God says, 'I will curse their blessings'—This is heresy!

"The priest's Mass is of no use for the dead, as one cannot prove there is a Purgatory. It is due to the avarice of the priests who have invented it, so as to draw to themselves earthly riches. Without money they will pray neither for the living nor the dead.

"Christ and His disciples were poor, they despised worldly riches. The Pope violently seizes upon these goods, and dissipates them in a shameful manner, when he ought to give them to the poor.

"Everyone, be he priest or layman, should marry, notwithstanding his vows. This is better than to lead a scandalous life."

These "errors" and still more were laid to the charge of John and his companions. In vain they defended themselves with passages from the Holy Scriptures. Once again they were asked, "Do you persist in your faith?" They replied without hesitation, "Yes, we do." Then they were conducted outside the town, near to the cemetery of St. Gall, amidst the lamentations of their sorrowing friends and relations, and they were forced to descend into a large and deep pit, lined on all sides with fagots. For a certain time the sound of Psalm singing arose out of the midst of the smoke and flames; then the voices of the martyrs became faint, till at last the silence of death reigned over this place of horror; people for centuries called it the "Pit of the heretics."

This "auto-da-fè" did not uproot the Gospel in Strasburg. It continued to be read in secret; it was explained and practiced in the society called "The Friends of God," out of which issued the most celebrated and consecrated preacher of the Middle ages, Jean Tauler. Already for many years taught by the Spirit, he had preached the religion of the heart, instead of external ceremonies. The people called him "Good Father Tauler." But he had not yet come to the full possession of the truth, and he did not attain to it till the venerable Nicolas of Bâle, chief of all "The Friends of God" of the upper Rhine, went to Strasburg to open the eyes of this celebrated preacher, and to put him face to face with the full light of the Gospel.

Tauler was offended and angry when Nicolas showed him his errors. The latter said that his temper was precisely a proof that he was seeking his own glory more than that of God.

Tauler exclaimed, "Truly you are the first to show me my deficiencies. I will henceforth, with the help of God and your counsel, reform my life. Be my spiritual guide, and let me be your disciple." Nicolas promised to give him some very simple advice. "Learn first to break your own will, and to obey the voice of God. Do not look behind you, nor be concerned with man, but think continually on the life and words of Christ, and regulate your life according to them." He counseled him to abandon preaching for some years and to make a profound study of the Bible.

It was a severe trial to Tauler, and one which drew upon him mockery and humiliation from the monks of his order. He fell ill and came to know poverty and misery, but he kept firm in this hard school. He sought and found peace, so that he could say, "Provided that I possess Thee, I am not disquieted by anything either in heaven or on earth." Nicholas exhorted him to continue in this peace, and permitted him again to take up preaching, and to show the Christians the true way to obtain eternal life. "It is no longer necessary," he told him, "for me to counsel you, since you have found the true Master, of whom I have been only the instrument. Obey Him, this is my last advice." From this time Tauler made rapid progress in Divine life, and increased more and more in the grace of the Holy Spirit.

The "New Church," Strasburg. Destroyed by fire in 1871.

The vast nave of the so-called "New Church" hardly sufficed to contain the number of the faithful who desired to listen to his preaching. The effect he produced on them was so powerful that it was not rare to see his auditors fall down fainting. The Pope forbade him to preach, but he gave no heed. Tauler would have been in a bad position if the town council had not protected him. When the plague ravaged the town, he was seen amidst the sick and dying, consoling them and administering the sacraments.

Luther said, speaking of his sermons, "he did not know any, either in German or Latin, the theology of which was more evangelical!" This is why Luther brought out again the little volume of which we reproduce the title page: "German Theology." If it was not written by Tauler himself, it was certainly issued from the circle of "The Friends of God." It sums up the Gospel better than any other work of the Middle ages.

Eyn geyſtlich edles Buchleynn.
von rechter vnderſcheyd
vnd vorſtand.was der
alt vñ new menſche ſey.Was Adams
vñ was gottis kind ſey.vñ wie Adã
ynn vns ſterben vnnd Chriſtus
erſteen ſall.

Title page of "German Theology."

V.

REFORMATION TIMES

V.

Reformation Times

he Middle Ages were coming to a close: with the Reformation a new era began. The Vaudois in their Valleys were filled with astonishment on learning what Luther had done in Germany, and Zwingli in Switzerland. They could not believe that this precious Word of God, which they alone in the center of Christianity had preserved from generation to generation, notwithstanding dangers and persecutions, should now be freely preached in many places, and that thousands of people should welcome this Book, by Rome condemned and proclaimed heretical! The news was too good to be admitted at the very outset. But other travelers confirmed it, and at last the Vaudois were forced to yield to their evidence. The Almighty had a second time said, "Let there be Light." The Light appeared, and its brightness filled many hearts. They acknowledged the true Savior; to Him they went to obtain pardon for their sins, life and salvation. That most shameful abuse of holy things, the commerce of "Indulgences" by Tetzel, had been a means to serve

God's plans, and to restore to Christianity the lost treasure of the Gospel.

As soon as the inhabitants of the Vaudois Valleys doubted no longer the accomplished fact, they sent deputies across the Alps to commune with the Reformers on the principal points of their common Faith. The messengers, the "Barbes" Martin of the Val de Luserna, George Morel, and Pierre Masson of Provence, were heartily welcomed wherever they went. At Zurich they saw Zwingli, and at Bâle, Ecolampadius and Capiton, and at Strasburg, Bucer. All these men gave thanks to God for having permitted this little troop of unlearned mountaineers the grace to preserve for centuries the true worship of God, as did in times past the seven thousand in the time of Elijah, who would not bow the knee to Baal.

The Reformers endeavored in their cordial conversations to explain many points of doctrine which they had not fully grasped, and when the delegates returned home they were inflamed with the desire to tell their compatriots and co-religionists all that they had learned and heard in foreign parts.

These Vaudois delegates assembled in the year 1532 in the wild valley of Angrogna. Some even came from the far away mountains of Calabria, where from ancient times the Vaudois had been established; and from Switzerland arrived Farel and Olivetan. Those were days of benediction; a new epoch commenced for the Vaudois with this Synod

The Valley of Angrogna.

at Angrogna. The principal articles of their Confession of Faith were discussed in fraternal conferences, invoking the aid of the Holy Spirit. The result of the deliberations formed the Church basis of all the Vaudois communities. No essential change of doctrine was necessary, but two important decisions were taken.

Firstly, worship was no longer to take place in secret, but in all the regularly constituted parishes each was to have its own pastor. Up till this time the elder "Barbes" had only been itinerant preachers. On the other hand, they were no longer to attend Mass—which till then had not been considered culpable—seeing that the adoration of the Host is contrary to the Word of God, and all hypocrisy should be renounced.

Secondly, to Olivetan was given the charge of preparing a new translation of the Bible for the Vaudois, as the old one was faulty. The poor mountaineers gave Olivetan five hundred golden crowns for the printing of this Bible at Neuchatel, whence it was to be distributed in the Valleys.

The Vaudois clearly perceived that by these decisions they would awaken the anger and enmity of Rome; but having become strong through brotherly fellowship, and confident in their Lord and Savior, they were ready to face everything, so as to confess—more openly than in the past—their faith before men. Their enemies tried hard to crush this revival of religious life. Here and there the

Vaudois had to defend themselves. In the 16th century a few witnesses shed their blood for their faith, such as Catalan Girardet, of San Giovanne de Lucerna, who was condemned to the stake in 1535. As soon as he was attached to the stake he made them bring him two stones, and cried out in a loud voice: "Poor people, who believe that by persecution like this you are able to exterminate our Church! Truly you are as incapable of it as I am of eating these stones!"

However, these persecutions were isolated; the wars which were going on between France and Savoy gave the Vaudois a relatively long time of repose.

These two powers were equally hostile to the Gospel, but their political quarrels left them no leisure to occupy themselves with religious questions. France conquered Piedmont and Savoy, and took good care not to alienate her new subjects by vexations. The Evangelical doctrine could thus spread under the aegis of the French arms. In the Valleys one after another rallied to this banner, and even Turin, the capital of the country, witnessed the formation of a flourishing Vaudois community, and some churches were constructed. Up till then, worship had been held in houses, in the open air, or in the chestnut forests. This was a time of progress and expansion such as the Vaudois Church had not yet known. They could hope that soon the Gospel banner would triumphantly wave on both sides of the Alps.

From Geneva, thanks to the tireless activity of that man of God named John Calvin, and of William Farel, his predecessor, a powerful current of spiritual life spread in the Latin countries.

The year 1559 brought a change. The victories of the Spanish troops obliged France to give up all her recent conquests; she had to surrender to the House of Savoy Piedmont and Savoy. Singularly enough, while the Vaudois under the scepter of the foreigner enjoyed relative repose, to the return of their legitimate Prince they were indebted for a time of severe trial. Emanuel Philibert of Savoy was an intimate friend of the terrible Spanish king, Philip II, surnamed "the Devil of the South." No Prince had ever persecuted the Evangelicals like him. Philibert had hardly returned to his country when he promulgated an Edict severely forbidding them to attend preaching which was other than Roman Catholic. Those who infringed this command would be fined one hundred crowns. The repetition of the offence would involve sentence to the galleys for life. This Edict fell like a bomb on the peaceable inhabitants of the Valleys. They immediately sent delegates to the Prince's Court, with a respectful petition, in which they said:

"Most Serene Highness!

It will ever be true, 'Heaven and earth will pass away, but My words will not pass away.' Now if our Faith be God's pure Word, of which we are fully convinced,

John Calvin.

William Farel.

and not human work, no earthly power will ever be able to destroy it.

Your Serene Highness knows but too well how terrible were the persecutions that have been undertaken for many years everywhere against the adherents of our Faith, but instead of discouraging or even exterminating them, they were strengthened and grew in number. Is not this sufficient proof and testimony that the matter is not man's but God's?

The Turks, Jews, heathen, and even savage people live up to their own religion, and no one tries to dissuade them from it by force. But we who serve the Almighty God and our sole Master and Redeemer Jesus Christ truly and faithfully, and have the same Gospel and baptism that you have, are not tolerated.

We beseech your Serene Highness, knowing your piety, and entreat you for the sake of our Savior and Redeemer to keep and protect us, your most obedient and most faithful subjects, in our sincere and pure faith, and not compel us to do things contrary to our consciences.

For the granting of our prayer we shall not cease to implore God on our knees daily to preserve your Serene Highness in health to your highest age!"

But their prayers and supplications were useless. To extirpate heresy the Duke, urged on by the Pope and Lainez, the General of the Jesuits, sent an army of from six to seven thousand men to the Valleys, who were further reinforced by French troops. Force and stratagem succeeded in taking Torre Pellice, chief town of the Vaudois, as well as a certain number of villages.

The prisoners endured inhuman cruelties. At Angrogna they bound a man of sixty years old to a table, cut open his abdomen, and fixed in the wound a receptacle full of insects, which penetrated into his body, and tortured him to death with fearful sufferings. To escape the brutal violence of the soldiers the young girls threw themselves over precipices, and all who could fly went to almost inaccessible mountains and caves. In despair, the men

Vaudois taking refuge in a cave. (After Jean Leger)

General view of Torre Pellice.

The Pillage of Torre Pellice. (After Jean Leger)

took up arms, withdrew into the natural fortresses of the country, where their valor made them well able to resist the enemy, and inflicted such marked losses on the latter that, after a year of desperate conflict, the Duke acknowledged that it was impossible to conquer this gallant little people. He consented to treat with them, and a formal peace was concluded at Cavor, on the 5th July, 1561. This treaty of peace, for the first time, assured them a certain amount of liberty of religion and conscience. They were permitted to assemble in their usual places to preach and to hold worship. Their pastors had the right to visit their sick, even beyond the Valleys, but they were not allowed to hold meetings, not even at Torre Pellice, nor Villars, where the Duke had fortresses erected. On the other hand, in all parishes where the Vaudois held worship, the Mass was to be said in concert.

The fugitives were given permission to return and rebuild their ruined houses. Though these rights and liberties appear to us to be narrowly limited, the Vaudois were profoundly grateful, their religion being at last legally recognized.

The treaty of Cavor, often broken afterwards, remained, up to the 19th century, the legal basis of the Vaudois Church.

In the following years the Duke, instigated by the Papists, again promulgated severe edicts against his best subjects. In 1565 he ordered that all those who refused to live according to the Roman Faith were, in two months' time, to leave his States, under pain of death and confiscation of their goods. The Vaudois formed a league, they swore obedience to the Duke and to the authorities, "for all his commands according to divine right and civil right, and as far as this was in conformity to the Word of God." On the other hand, they promised each other mutual aid and counsel in every circumstance.

After that they appealed for the intervention of the Duchess, who favored them, and to the Elector Palatine. These efforts succeeded beyond their hopes. The severe edicts were partly revoked, and partly abandoned, so that during the life of Duke Philibert the Vaudois Church was relatively quiet. This Prince's wise administration benefited the country, and he left an honored name.

Under his successors, obstacles and acts of violence were not wanting. However, the long wars with France and Spain occupied the Dukes elsewhere. More than once the Vaudois valiantly defended the Alpine passes, and thus rendered great services to their country. Thus they obtained some repose. This did not prevent the priests from employing allurements and artifice to make them renounce their faith. Sometimes it would be a rich marriage, sometimes impunity for some misdoing. A young Vaudois allowed himself to be drawn into stealing precious objects from the Catholic Cathedral at Torre Pellice. Usually the profanation of a church was punished with death. He promised to attend Mass, and the affair was hushed up.

The Archbishop of Turin came with a brilliant suite to dazzle the inhabitants by a display of Roman pomp and splendor. The Capucines and Jesuits inundated the Valleys, using every means to make proselytes. They attached themselves especially to those who were suffering some ecclesiastical penalty, or some law suit with their neighbors, but their conquests were very trifling.

A writer of this time, named Brez, declared that "Of all the Vaudois who had ever abjured, he did not know of one who had done so from conviction; the cause was always either passion, profit, or crime."

The Vaudois Valleys were devastated in 1630 by that terrible epidemical disease, the plague. All the pastors, excepting two, were victims of the devotion with which they visited the sick and dying. The Catholics rejoiced, hoping to make an easy prey of a shepherdless flock. But from Geneva, and France, where the Huguenots lived in peace under the Edict of Nantes, they easily obtained substitutes for those whom death had taken away.

Rome understood that other measures were necessary to conquer this fortress of the faith, and she did not hesitate to set them going.

VI.

THE YEAR 1655

VI.
The Year 1655

ll that we have recounted is surpassed in horror by the terrible doings of the year 1655. This date is inscribed in letters of blood in the history of the Vaudois.

There had been instituted not long before, at Turin, a branch of the "Congregation for the Propagation of the Faith, and the Extermination of Heresy." "This was the most terrible battery ever set up against our poor ancestors," said a Vaudois historian, because this society, with which the foremost personages of the Court were associated, took such measures that the feeble Duke, Charles Emanuel II, gave his consent to a diabolical plan conceived by the Marquis de Pinasse. This latter, at the head of an army of sixteen thousand men, entered the Valleys under the pretext of protecting the frontiers.

He persuaded the principal men of the villages to give a proof of their attachment to the Duke by receiving the soldiers into their houses for several days. On the faith of solemn promises the unhappy people gave their consent. Suddenly, on the morning of the twenty-fourth of April, a signal previously agreed upon was heard from the heights of Castella, near Torre Pellice, when the soldiers fell on their unsuspecting hosts, crying out, "Down with these dogs!" Then commenced a butchery, a pillage, and a destruction by fire and sword, which defies all description.

Men and women, children and old people, were all murdered without distinction. The bestial madness of the soldiers was not satisfied by immolating their victims, but the torturers invented unheard of torments. Babes were impaled on their mother's breasts, or broken on the rocks before their eyes. Women and young girls were mutilated, violated, and slowly put to death by unspeakable means. Men were dragged up the steep rock which dominates Torre Pellice, and precipitated into the abyss. Into the mouths of others they put powder and set it alight, the explosion shattering the skull and scattering afar their brains.

I neither can, nor will recount all the horrors and infamous acts perpetrated on their defenseless victims by these demons with human faces. Pastor Jean Leger, Moderator of the Vaudois Church, has handed them on to posterity according to accounts of ocular witnesses, stating accurately the names, the dates, and the circumstances. This document is a monument to the undying shame of the murderers, and of those who urged them on in the name of religion; and one of glory to those who,

Vaudois thrown over a precipice. (After Jean Leger)

notwithstanding all the martyrdom it entailed, continued steadfast in the Faith.

Jean Léger.

Daniel Rambaut preferred to have his fingers cut off, one after the other, rather than recite an "Ave Maria." The peasant Jean Paillas' attention was called to the fate that awaited his wife and eleven children after his death. "I ask for them no other mercy," said he, "than to follow in my steps." Women vied with men in their courage, and marched to death singing hymns.

The storm fell so suddenly, that towns and villages were pillaged and burnt before the inhabitants could defend themselves. The soldiers went in chase of the fugitives, and more than one piece of human game was shot before it could reach the protection of the mountain retreats. Everywhere, on the roadsides, in the streets, in the fields, the corpses of the victims were lying; impaled on the

Title Page of Jean Leger's Book, "Histoire des Vaudois du Piémont."

fences were to be seen their detached heads and members. In the solitudes women wandered, calling in vain their murdered husbands; and children searched for their mothers who were no more. They who had continued for centuries seemed to be exterminated at a single blow.

But the enemy triumphed too soon. Over four thousand harmless people were destroyed in this terrible carnage, two thousand died of hunger and cold. However, a number of Vaudois in the distant Valleys had been able to fly into the mountains and entrench themselves, and there they defended their country to the last drop of blood, and revenged the death of their brothers. They assembled in an eagle's nest called Rora. The leader of this desperate troop was *Joshua Janavel*; he, when given notice of the order to give himself up and to attend Mass within twenty-four hours, exclaimed, "Rather death than the Mass." This little troop held out against several thousand soldiers, retiring from one valley to another, further and further into the mountains. The arrival of fugitives and co-religionists from France augmented their numbers to such an extent that they in their turn could attack the enemy, put them to flight, reconquer several villages by sudden attacks, and keep their foes in check.

In the meantime the rumor of this abominable crime which these quiet Alpine valleys had witnessed was spread abroad in Europe, arousing everywhere indignation and horror. In the Protestant countries it evoked profound sympathy, and started an admirable movement of practical charity. Switzerland, the nearest country, brought the first relief. The evangelical Cantons appointed a day of fasting and humiliation, organized collections, and sent to the Duke of Savoy a deputation, composed of their most prominent magistrates, supplicating him to spare

JOSUE JANAVEL

his subjects. Holland was not less active. In Amsterdam eighty-six thousand crowns were collected in a single day in favor of the persecuted Vaudois. Other towns followed this noble example. The Grand Elector of Brandenburg interceded in their favor.

The ruler who agitated with most success was Oliver Cromwell,* Lord Protector of England.

He gave £2000 out of his private purse, and ordered his Ambassador at Paris to remonstrate most strongly at the French Court on the subject of the atrocities which the government had allowed to be committed quite close to its frontier, and moreover with the concurrence of the French troops.

At Paris they knew Cromwell well enough to be aware that he was capable of taking up arms in favor of his co-religionists. So the Court of Turin was advised to abate its severity towards the Vaudois. The Duke of Savoy, seeing that he could not resist the demands of the Protestant States of Europe, substituted perfidy for violence, and

---

* The following is a translation of a Latin letter Cromwell wrote to the Genevan Senate in 1655, which shows the deep interest he took in the persecuted Vaudois:

> "Oliver, Protector of England, Scotland, and Ireland, to the illustrious Senate of the free State of Geneva, Greeting, Most Illustrious and Eminent Men, our very dear friends.

> The very melancholy intelligence which has reached us of the bloody massacre of those of the Evangelical religion inhabiting the Alpine Valleys, and the imminent danger which in consequence hangs over the Protestant Faith, has made so deep an impression on our minds, and filled us, and still continues to fill us, with such intense solicitude, that we have dispatched our faithful and beloved

made a hypocritical peace. In the Edict of Grace, at Rivoli, he renewed most of the privileges which had been already granted in the peace of Cavor. But he determined not to hold to the promise given. The Vaudois were, as in the past, tormented and oppressed. The garrison of Torre Pellice, in particular, made no scruple in maltreating the Protestants of the town and neighborhood. They pillaged, extorted money, and committed violence of all kinds, so that at last the Protestants abandoned their houses, seeking shelter in the most retired places.

The spiritual leaders of the Vaudois, and, in particular, the excellent pastor Jean Leger, were banished from the country as traitors. On renewed representations from the foreign Ambassadors, reply was made that this was a case of rebellion, and it was necessary to reduce to obedience those who were in revolt against established authority. In reality they had brought these poor persecuted ones to such a state of exasperation in destroying their houses,

George Downing, John Pel, our resident at Genoa, Samuel Morland, Gent., extraordinary Commissioners, to lay before you our feelings on this subject. Therefore we entreat you to vouchsafe to them a free audience and entire confidence in the communications which they shall make to you from us. Ending with which we desire to commend you to the protection of the Supreme Ruler.

From our Hall at Westminster, July 29th, 1655.

Your good friend,

OLIVER, P."

(Note by the translator).

their crops, and by other unqualifiable acts, that they—who only demanded to live in peace—for the second time took up arms, under the leadership of the valiant Janavel, to protect their families and their homes. They gained victories over the Duke's troops at Torre Pellice and Angrogna, and won so many successes in this little war, the scene of which was their well known mountains, that the Duke became weary of a struggle both ruinous and useless. At about this time his mother, Christine, and his wife, the Duchesse Françoise (who had been the most active in stirring him up against the heretics), died within a short time of each other.

In the latter years of his life he left his poor subjects in peace, permitted them to rebuild their ruined houses, to cultivate their fields which had gone to waste, and to replant chestnut trees, which in the most remote valleys was the principal means of sustenance for the people.

Alas ! this peace was not of long duration. To the memory of the innumerable victims of that terrible year, whose names no tombstone, no monument has preserved, Milton's famous complaint may follow here.

ON THE LATE MASSACRE IN PIEDMONT.
"Avenge, Oh Lord, Thy slaughtered saints, whose bones
Lie scattered on the Alpine mountains cold:
Even them who kept Thy truth so pure of old

The Year 1655

When all our fathers worshipped stocks and stones,
Forget not! in Thy book record their groans,
Who were Thy sheep, and in their ancient fold
Slain by the bloody Piedmontese that rolled
Mother and infant down the rocks. Their moans
The vales redoubled to the hills, and they
To Heaven. Their martyred blood and ashes sow
Over all the Italian fields, where still doth sway
The triple tyrant: that from these may grow
A hundredfold, who having learned Thy way
Early may fly the Babylonian woe."

VII.

HENRI ARNAUD AND THE GLORIOUS RETURN

Henri Arnaud.

VII.
Henri Arnaud and the Glorious Return

n 1685 Louis XIV revoked the Edict of Nantes, and prohibited all exercise of the Protestant religion in his States. Thousands on thousands of Huguenots were obliged to leave their country. As the King feared that the Huguenots of the South of France would find succor and support with the Vaudois, their near neighbors, he stirred up the mind of the youthful Duke Victor Amadeus II, of Savoy, and persuaded him to come to the same resolution. He even went so far as to threaten to send an army of fourteen thousand men to chase the Vaudois from their Valleys, and to seize the territory for himself. As early as the month of January, 1686, the Duke issued a law similar in all points to that of the Revocation in France. Their common origin was evident. In this deed the religious tolerance, formerly accorded, was solemnly revoked. All acts of evangelical worship were strictly prohibited, even in private houses. The churches and chapels of the Vaudois were to be razed to the ground. All pastors and teachers who would not become Catholics were to leave the country in fourteen days, under pain of death and confiscation of their goods.

Those who became converts would continue to receive their salaries, augmented by a fourth. All children for the future were to be baptized Catholics. In case of resistance on the part of the parents, the father was to be punished by five years on the galleys, and the mother beaten with rods.

Every clause was a crushing blow to these courageous confessors. This time the remonstrances of the Evangelical Cantons and of the Princes of Germany remained without effect. Strengthened by the support of France, which had already dispatched to the Valleys an army of ten thousand men under the command of the celebrated Catinat, the Court of Turin refused all concession. From two sides powerful armies were advancing towards these mountains, which had been so often the scene of abominable devastations. This time the attempt was bound to succeed. Good leaders, unity, and decision were lacking to the Vaudois. Some of their troops were taken by stratagem; they were promised the permission to go away free if they would give up their arms, instead of which they were made prisoners.

The last mountain fortress, Pra-del-Tor, which had resisted so many assaults, was taken; a few cannon dragged by mules up the neighboring heights quickly overthrew the roughly made entrenchments, and routed the defenders.

That which the enemies of the Vaudois sought so long without obtaining, they held at last.

All the Vaudois Valleys up to the summits of the mountains were in the Duke's hands, the inhabitants were vanquished, annihilated, or prisoners, from three thousand to four thousand had perished, and about fourteen thousand were made prisoners and put into jail. The remainder wandered aimlessly in the mountains, or took refuge in Switzerland. The silence of death reigned in these Valleys, which were soaked in blood. Only smoking ruins marked the sites where the pious inhabitants had labored and worshipped, and two thousand children were torn from their parents and placed in Catholic families to be brought up in the Roman faith. The fate of the prisoners was so terrible that in less than a year five thousand of them died.

When the Swiss learned of this unspeakable distress, they sent deputies to the Duke, beseeching him to permit the prisoners to emigrate. The maintenance and supervision of so many thousands, who held out notwithstanding the bad treatment and all attempts to convert them, was a burdensome charge in the long run. Nevertheless the Duke hesitated for a long time. He waited till the end of November, when the Alpine chain was already covered with deep snow, and the autumn winds rendered the journey arduous. Did he conceive the diabolical plan, by means of cold and snow, to finish what hunger and sword had spared? The clothing of the emigrants was so bad, and they had so little provision, that a number of them perished in the snow on Mont Cenis, not less than eighty-six in one day alone.

At the Swiss frontier a cordial welcome awaited them; they were given refreshments, and provided with good warm rugs to protect them from the icy blasts of the wind. When the lamentable procession—which resembled a funeral march—approached Geneva, all the members of the Town Council went to meet and salute these heroes of the Faith. The citizens vied with each other in zeal to receive into their houses, and to succor these poor ones, even though the town was already inundated with French refugees.

One can never appreciate highly enough what Geneva, Bern, and Bale, and in general all the Evangelical Cantons of Switzerland, did for these Martyrs. A great many of the fugitives could not remain in Switzerland. As soon as the winter was over they continued their route towards the north, and under the Protestant princes in Wurtemberg, Hesse, the Palatinate and Brandenburg, they found new homes where they could live in peace, serving their Lord according to their conscience.

Then a singular phenomenon happened. The terrible sufferings which they had endured in their mountains had only rendered the same more dear to their hearts, and in foreign countries they were consumed with home sickness. Unhappy in their security, they longed to return to the places where they were born. This state of things occasioned an audacious project to spring up in the mind of Pastor Henri Arnaud, who had already conducted several companies of Vaudois to Wurtemberg, and there established them.

He, like the refugees, could not become acclimatized in a foreign country, and he wished to return with them to Piedmont, and, taking arms in their hands, reconquer their native soil. He was better qualified than any other for such a venturesome enterprise. In his youth he had served in Holland, and had attained to the grade of captain. William of Orange, the powerful protector of Protestants, esteemed him highly. The obstacles to this project were numberless. The Vaudois had to observe the greatest secrecy, so that their departure should not be hindered by their respective governments. Notwithstanding all the precautions taken, the projects got abroad. All could not get away; only about eight hundred or nine hundred Vaudois arrived at the previously agreed on meeting place, which was on the shore of Lake Geneva, near Prangins.

It was on the night of the 16th of August, 1689. There, Arnaud and his companions fell on their knees and "besought God, who in old times led Israel through the Red Sea, and brought them back to the land of their fathers, to go before them like a pillar of cloud, and with His All-Powerful arm to open up a way for them through their enemies."

Embarkation of the Vaudois at Prangins. (After a lithograph by J. Hebert.)

A few boats transported them to the opposite side of the Lake, where they commenced to climb the mountains of Savoy. Marching was very difficult, because it was necessary to avoid the highways, so as not to be betrayed. They hastened to cross the Mont Cenis by perilous paths. It was raining in torrents, but, notwithstanding, they continued their way, so as to avoid being overtaken by the Savoy troops. But they had been discovered. As they descended from Mont Cenis to the valley of Susa, near the bridge of Salabertrand, which crosses the torrent of Dora, they were received by the hot fire of twenty-five hundred well-equipped soldiers.

Arnaud ordered his men to throw themselves flat on the ground, and the balls whistled over their heads without harming them. At this moment they perceived behind them companies of their enemies, who had thus caught them between two fires, at which those in the first rank rushed in advance shouting, "Courage, comrades! the bridge is ours!" Their attack was so impetuous that the enemy, driven out, fled crying, "Sauve qui peut."

The Savoy troops lost six hundred men in this action, while the Vaudois had only fifteen dead to lament. The news of this extraordinary victory outstripped them, and wherever they went they were allowed to pass without being troubled. As a measure of precaution, at each place they took away a hostage, some one of note, a noble, priest, or monk. They observed strict discipline, and paid

The Battle on the Bridge of Salabertrand.

for the bread and meat which the peasants handed over to them.

At the foot of Monte Piso they encountered for the second time a troop of Piedmontese, which they repulsed. At last, after ten days of uninterrupted marching, climbing, and combats, they arrived at their native Valleys, and held their first service at Prali. Arnaud preached a moving sermon on Psalm 129:2-4: "Many a time have they afflicted me from my youth; yet they have not prevailed against me. The plowers plowed upon my back; they made long their furrows. The Lord is righteous; He hath cut asunder the cords of the wicked." This text might be applied to them nearly word for word.

But the hardest part of their task was still before them. From east and west the soldiers of Piedmont and France were approaching to surround, with a circle of iron, and crush this audacious band, which dared to resist two powerful princes. On Sunday, the 1st September, the Vaudois met together at Sibaaud, above the village of Bobbio. There, one after another, the men, leaders and common soldiers, swore mutual fidelity till death, and never to separate or divide.

"Since the mercy of God has happily brought us back to the heritage of our Fathers, to reestablish here the true worship of our holy religion, we have decided to terminate the great work that the All-Powerful God has till now marvelously directed in our favor. We each and all promise our Lord and Savior Jesus Christ to consecrate all our strength to deliver our brothers, the prisoners of cruel Babylon, and to reconstruct with them the Kingdom of our Lord, and to defend it to the death."

Arnaud read this oath, and the entire troop repeated it, while they raised their right hands. This was the "Rütli" of the Vaudois, and here their sun of liberty arose.

When, on the two hundredth anniversary of the "Rimpatrio," as the Return is called in Italian, they raised a simple monument to the memory of their ancestors, they inscribed on it the names of all the Vaudois parishes.

To avoid being invested and destroyed by the enemy's troops, Arnaud and his followers, at the commencement of winter, retired to a fortified position called Balsiglia. Behind, the mountain chain of the Hautes Alps and the rock of the Quatre Dents protected them. In front opened the impracticable valley of San Martino, traversed by the rapid torrent of the Germanasca. There they dug out caves in the earth, and surrounded the place with a circle of entrenchments, in terraces one above the other, which would command the enemy in every direction.

On account of the war troubles, and a premature fall of snow, the inhabitants of the neighboring hamlets had been unable to harvest the poor crops of wheat. Under the protecting snow they were found intact and ground into flour, and this furnished abundant provision for the besieged. The enemy was already advancing: ten thousand

The Monument of Sibaaud.

Valley of the Germanasca.

The Balsiglia.

French soldiers, under the command of Marshal Catinat; twelve thousand Piedmontese, in all twenty-two thousand men. To prevent escape they occupied the villages, the heights, and the passes, thinking they could easily reduce this handful of besieged, who now, after so many skirmishes, hardly numbered four hundred men.

But they had calculated badly. When the ramparts were thrown up, Arnaud had placed branches and thorns, turned outwards, between stones. The assaulting troops getting entangled in these, whole ranks fell under the hot fire of the Vaudois. The succeeding assaults had no better success, and Colonel de Parat, while conducting the troops, was himself taken prisoner. The small village of Balsiglia was destroyed by the enemy, a neighboring mill was burnt, but the fortress itself was impregnable.

It was now the turn for menace and promises. They tried to make them see the uselessness of resistance against the all-powerful King of France. If they would surrender, they were told, they would be allowed to return to Switzerland and receive five hundred louis in gold for the journey, otherwise they would all be run through with the sword. "We are not subjects of the King of France," they replied. "The King of France is not the master of this country, therefore we cannot enter into negotiations with his troops. With the help of the God of armies, we will live and die in the heritage of our fathers."

Catinat was furious that his military science had come to naught before such a wretched nest in the rocks, and he decided on a regular siege. He requisitioned all the peasants in the neighborhood, and forced them to make a road through the rocks, at great cost, to bring up his cannon.

While the artillery bombarded the fortress, making gaping breaches in the primitive earthworks, pioneers climbed to the ridge of the mountain, barricaded every conquered place by means of redoubts, and approached nearer and nearer to the besieged. These latter defended themselves with courage, each of their sorties inflicting serious loss on the enemy, but nevertheless they were obliged to abandon, one after the other, the earthworks they had thrown up. At length, narrowly shut in, they had nothing but the prospect of death before their eyes. Catinat's troops had climbed the mountain behind them, thus cutting off all possibility of retreat. They resolved to hold out to the last man, and to sell their lives as dearly as possible. They prepared themselves for death.

At this moment, when all hope seemed lost, one of the Vaudois leaders remembered, that when he was a child seeking some lost goats, he had descended to the bed of the torrent through a fissure in the rocks on his hands and feet. During a thick fog which God spread over the mountain, they ventured to descend this break-neck chasm with bare feet, so as not to slip, or make any noise which might betray them. Suddenly one of them let fall his kettle, which rebounded with a crash from rock to rock. The sentinel on the other side cried out "Qui vive?" Not obtaining any answer, he became quiet. The little company made a way through the rocks in the torrent, entered a lateral gorge, and was saved!

Next morning, when the French undertook a final and decisive assault, they found the nest empty. The birds had flown! Overcome with fury they dashed in pursuit of the fugitives, hunting them over hill and dale. God himself put an end to this furious chase.

While Arnaud was defending the Balsiglia all through the winter up to the month of May, important changes had taken place in the political world. Duke Amadeus, angry with Louis XIV, who was treating him as a vassal and not as an ally, joined the European coalition, the object of which was to curb the insatiable ambition of the King of France. The allies of yesterday became the enemies of today. The Duke desired to see the French troops evacuate the country as quickly as possible. To accomplish this the concurrence of Arnaud, his heroic band, and of the other Vaudois who lived here and there hidden in the ravines, was welcomed.

The Duke set at liberty the prisoners, and released those on the galleys; from Switzerland, the Palatinate, Wurtemberg, and Brandenburg he recalled his fugitive subjects, and sent them to shed their blood and give their lives for a prince who had nearly annihilated them!

Arnaud's auxiliary troops rendered signal services in the wars against France, the leader was praised and the men were given the assurance of civil and religious liberty by solemn treaty.

However, if they hoped at last to enjoy repose, and be able to live according to their faith, they were terribly deceived. The Court of Turin did not scruple to make treaties and to break them soon afterwards, to publish solemn edicts only to revoke them after a few years.

The Duke being hard pressed by the French, sought refuge with the Vaudois, and lived among them for a certain time in the little village of Rora, but as soon as he was no longer in straits he forgot his oaths and the benefits he had received, and, according to the custom of his ancestors, he began again to torment and oppress the people. Some of those who had come to his help had a second time to take the path of exile, on the pretext that they had been born on French territory.

Henri Arnaud was himself expelled. They brought an action for high treason against him, notwithstanding the intervention of the Protestant powers. William of Orange wished to attract him to his court, and give him a splendid position, with the title of Colonel, but the worthy man preferred to suffer the affliction with the people of God rather than to live in the favor and luxury of a king's court. He used to advantage the high regard he enjoyed in the Protestant world to alleviate, as far as possible, the lot of his compatriots who had taken refuge in foreign countries.

In the newly-established Vaudois settlement of Schöneberg in Wurtemberg, he established himself, and there again labored as a simple pastor for twelve years. His new country owed to him the introduction of the potato, which from old times they had cultivated in the Valleys, but which was till then unknown in Suabia. There he died in the peace of God, at the age of eighty, on the 8th September, 1721, and was interred at the foot of the communion table in the simple village church. A slab of marble bears the following inscription:

"Here you see the ashes of Arnaud, but no one can show his work, his combats, and his invincible courage. Just as the son of Jesse fought the thousands of Philistines, he also held out alone, against the army and the chief of his enemies."

In place of the little old wooden church, a beautiful edifice in stone is now erected. The memory of Arnaud is held in honor and benediction in the hearts of all the Vaudois.

Interior of the ancient Vaudois Temple of Schöneberg (Wurtemberg) with Henri Arnaud's Tomb.

VIII.

THE VAUDOIS OF OUR TIMES

VIII.
The Vaudois of Our Times

e should have much more to tell if we were to recount all that happened to the Vaudois during the 18th and 19th centuries, but we need not unfold this endless chain of persecutions, of oppressions, of treaties sworn and broken, of civil and religious tyranny. It is enough to say that this people of iron and steel remained steadfastly attached to their faith, and were always constant to the House of Savoy, from which they had suffered so much.

Under the reign of Napoleon I, for fifteen years they enjoyed complete liberty and civic equality. For this declared enemy of Papacy knew how to appreciate their valor and their love of independence. As a General, Napoleon accorded to Arnaud's expedition unqualified admiration.

With the return of the legitimate sovereign, in 1815, recommenced the system of vexations, which the Great Powers could only put a stop to temporarily. Prussia, in particular, energetically concerned herself with the lot of the Vaudois. Count Waldburg-Truchsess, her ambassador at Turin, was their friend and indefatigable defender. On his death, in the year 1844, they wept for him as for a Father.

Another benefactor was our compatriot, General Beckwith. He had been obliged to resign the service of his King, having lost a leg in the glorious battle of Waterloo. Henceforth he consecrated his time and fortune to the service of the Heavenly King. By his personal liberality, and collections among his rich compatriots, he helped the Vaudois church to raise itself out of the precarious condition in which he found it, to build primary and secondary schools for boys and girls, to construct hospitals, and, in a word, to organize itself. He did more. By his residence in Torre Pellice from 1815, and by the influence of several friends and clergymen, he in time succeeded in vanquishing the rationalism which had penetrated into the Valleys, with the result that these ancient corporations of confessors had become torpid. He had the joy of seeing the faith of their fathers spring up again, and the missionary spirit become developed among the spiritual descendants of Peter Valdus.

When, in 1848, a new constitution swept away all secular restrictions, they went in a great procession through the streets of the capital to offer thanks to their King for having freed them from the serfdom of centuries. When they arrived at the palace, amidst the shouts of the entire people, they presented to the sovereign the Vaudois flag which had been so long proscribed, renewing at the same

Count Waldburg Truchsess.

General Beckwith.

time their oath of fidelity. Later, in the years 1859 and 1870, when the Gospel found access throughout the country, even including Rome, they unfolded another banner—that of the Gospel—showing their gratitude to their Lord and Savior, Who had so marvelously kept and delivered them. From Torre Pellice, from Perosa, from Angrogna, from Pomaretto, from all the places famous in their martyrology, they sent messengers to their compatriots, who were enslaved by human institutions and superstition, to carry to them the good news of the grace of God.

The old seal of the Vaudois, "Lux Lucet in Tenebris," *i.e.*, The Light shines in Darkness, regained its symbolical meaning. As far as it depended on them, they held aloft the lamp of faith. They endeavored, and are still seeking to enlighten all who dwell in their common country, Italy. With the help of England, Holland, Germany, and Switzerland, they founded at Florence a Theological College, with excellent professors; to name two—Professors Comba and Geymonat.

They established Vaudois communities at Turin, Milan, Leghorn, Genoa, and Naples, even at Rome; in Calabria and in Sicily they erected churches and schools, while their evangelists and colporteurs carried the Word of God to the villages and hamlets. They have become a Missionary Church throughout Italy, as General Beckwith predicted in 1848.

Perosa and Pomaretto.

Seal of the Vaudois Church,
"The Light Shines in Darkness."

Vaudois Church at Rome.

Vaudois Church at Turin.

Such a work is all the more difficult and necessary in a country where the immediate presence of the Papacy and the labors of the Jesuits have developed a crass superstition and materialistic atheism. The sower must patiently await the fertilizing rains, and continue his work without abatement.

At the present time the Vaudois Church numbers fifty parishes, a hundred stations, and fifteen colonies, where the Gospel is preached to the Italians. It is not necessary to say that the poor people of the Valleys are not able to support this extensive missionary work out of their own funds, but are assisted by considerable gifts made by the Christians of Protestant countries.

Their missionary zeal has carried them as far as Africa, where, in cooperation with "La Société des Missions de Paris," they work among the Basutos and the Barotses, on the banks of the Zambezi.

With the increase of the population emigration became necessary, the land of the Valleys being unable to supply food for more than a certain number, consequently some are turning their steps towards the large ports and commercial centers of the south of France, where their energy and honesty are appreciated. Others go further afield, and are founding colonies in North and South America, where with unremitting zeal they are maintaining the customs and faith of their ancestors.

Thus this little people has spread all over the world, as light-bearers here and there amidst the surrounding darkness, yet for all that the center of gravity remains still in the Valleys.

To conclude, it will be worthwhile for my readers, who have obligingly followed me through so many horrible events, to accompany me still further, and see these Valleys as they are at present. It will repay them the trouble, and the journey is not difficult, as the railway conducts us as far as Torre Pellice.

Though Italian is the official language, the people still use a strange medley of idioms. Most of them speak French according to ancient usage, while the old Vaudois patois has also been preserved in remote localities, which is closely allied to the Provencal of the Middle Ages.

Torre Pellice presents a similar diversity from a religious point of view. Half the population are Roman Catholics: these are the workers in the manufactories which have been erected one after another in this broad valley. The smoke from their lofty chimneys contrasts unpleasantly with the rural tranquility all round, with the vines propped on tall poles, and the glistening verdure of the fields of maize.

The stranger remarks with astonishment the houses roofed with immense flagstones.

A rocky point, from which many confessors were flung down, overhangs the town, and appears to menace as much as protect it.

At the foot of the hill are grouped the buildings forming the headquarters of the Vaudois Church. First the hospital, surrounded by a shady garden; a little below is the "Temple," a church both simple and dignified; opposite is the College, and to the right stands the "Maison des Vaudois." This latter building contains the Library and Museum, with its precious books, engravings, arms and moneys, which comprise the glorious history of this heroic people.

Every year the Synod, composed of the pastors and elders of the different parishes, meets to discuss and regulate communal affairs, for this Church, after having so long endured rigorous oppression, has now the right to direct itself without State interference in any way whatever. They themselves elect their supreme authority, called "La Table," which is composed of the most capable of their pastors and elders. Their duties consist in executing the decisions of the Synod, administering the finances, and regulating general affairs.

The society of these simple and worthy men is beneficial. The least show of interest in the history of their Church is appreciated, and they receive with brotherly cordiality those who visit them from foreign countries.

The Temple and Maison des Vaudois at Torre Pellice.

The Temple at Bobbio.

However great the pleasure experienced in conversing with them, we must go further if we would see a Vaudois parish of the ancient and authentic type. These are only to be found in the most elevated parts, where the whistle of the locomotive is not heard, and where the smoke from the chimneys of the manufactories has not yet penetrated; for example Bobbio, four hours higher up the mountains, at the termination of the Val de Lucerna.

Whoever has been privileged to join in a service of this village church, with its whitewashed walls, bare and undecorated, its heavy benches, and the ceiling supported by four squared columns, will never forget it.

Here they enter, these vigorous mountaineers, of dark complexion, their visage tanned by hardships. It would seem as if persecution had traced the many wrinkles on their faces. The women sit on one side. Their little caps, radiant with whiteness, make one think of an assembly of deaconesses. Some of them wear a black veil over the cap; these are in mourning. Thank God we see few of these, but two or three centuries ago how many were those who came here to mourn their husbands, brothers, or children.

But now the singing of the assembly is heard. It is sonorous and powerful. The voices fill the nave. From a small pulpit the schoolmaster reads a portion from the Gospels.

On remarking how seriously and devoutly they were listening to the sermon, I said to myself, "If the necessity presented itself again, these men and women also would sacrifice their goods and their lives for the Gospel. Is it not to fortify themselves in view of this possible sacrifice that they now approach the table of the Lord—consisting of a massive block of wood, over which was laid a coarse linen cloth—to receive the symbols of the body and blood of Christ, broken and poured out for the remission of the sins of many?"

As soon as the pastor had pronounced the words of Christ, an elder takes his place beside him and holds the cup, while the pastor breaks the bread, and the schoolmaster reads the passages selected from the Bible. The Lord's Supper is the same everywhere, and when it is received with faith, it always benefits and is a blessing. Nevertheless, a communion celebrated among the descendants of those who shed their blood to preserve this precious privilege is a memory which can never fade.

It was in this very church, of Bobbio, that Arnaud's men assembled to strengthen themselves in God before going up above to the hill of Sibaaud, where they swore to conquer or to die together.

Just as the dyke, built of indestructible rocks, which slants across the valley to divert from this quiet spot the devastating waters of the torrent, so those valiant men were the first to throw themselves across the menacing stream which in 1689 ravaged all these Valleys. With their bodies they set up at Balsiglia a dyke, against which the tide of Papal slavery and Roman superstition came and broke itself.

May the God of their fathers be with their descendants. May He fortify their spirit of sacrifice, augment their courage as witnesses, so that they may fulfill the high mission entrusted to them, and that their light may shine more and more in the darkness around.

FINIS

For further reading on the faith,
history, and persecutions of the Vaudois and
Waldensian Christians, visit us online at:
www.hailandfire.com

"By manifestation of the truth commending ourselves to
every man's conscience in the sight of God."
2 Corinthians 3:2

HAIL & FIRE

Hail & Fire is a resource for Reformed and Gospel Theology
in the works, exhortations, prayers, and apologetics of those
who have maintained the Gospel and expounded upon the
Scripture as the Eternal Word of God and the sole authority in
Christian doctrine.

For the edification of those who believe the Gospel in truth and
for the examination of all consciences, Hail & Fire reprints and
republishes, in print and online, Christian, Puritan, Reformed
and Protestant sermons and exhortative works; Protestant and
Catholic polemical and apologetical works; Bibles, histories,
martyrologies, and eschatological works.

Visit us online at:
www.hailandfire.com

www.ingramcontent.com/pod-product-compliance
Lightning Source LLC
Chambersburg PA
CBHW061730020426
42331CB00006B/1187